Lewis AND Clark

Meriwether Lewis

William Clark

SPIRIT
of America™

Lewis AND *Clark*

EXPLORERS

By Cynthia Klingel and Robert B. Noyed

The Child's World®
The Child's World®
Chanhassen, Minnesota

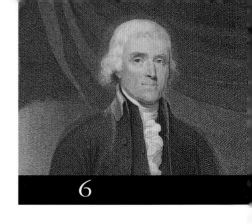

6

Lewis AND *Clark*

Published in the United States of America by The Child's World®
PO Box 326 • Chanhassen, MN 55317-0326 • 800-599-READ • www.childsworld.com

Acknowledgments
   The Child's World®: Mary Berendes, Publishing Director

   Editorial Directions, Inc.: E. Russell Primm, Emily Dolbear, and Lucia Raatma, Editors; Linda S. Koutris, Photo Selector; Dawn Friedman, Photo Research; Red Line Editorial, Fact Research; Irene Keller, Copy Editor; Tim Griffin/IndexServ, Indexer; Chad Rubel, Proofreader

Photos
   Cover: Independence National Historical Park; National Portrait Gallery, Smithsonian Institution/Art Resource, NY: 6, 28; Smithsonian American Art Museum, Washington, DC/Art Resource, NY: 14; photographer Gerard Blot, Reunion des Musees Nationaux/Art Resource, NY: 17; Private Collection/Bridgeman Art Library: 9; Library of Congress, Washington, DC/Bridgeman Art Library: 21 top; Burstein Collection/Corbis: 16; Historical Picture Archive/Corbis: 15 top, 25; Bettmann/Corbis, 15 bottom; Hulton Archive/Getty Images: 11; Independence National Historical Park: 2, 8; Library of Congress: 7; North Wind Picture Archives: 13, 18, 24, 26, 27; Stock Montage: 12, 19, 20, 21 bottom, 23.

Library of Congress Cataloging-in-Publication Data
   Klingel, Cynthia Fitterer.
   Lewis and Clark : explorers / by Cynthia Klingel and Robert B. Noyed.
      p. cm.
   Includes index.
   Summary: A brief account of the exploratory expedition led by Lewis and Clark across the little known territory from St. Louis to the Pacific Ocean in the early nineteenth century.
   ISBN 1-56766-164-5 (library bound : alk. paper)
   1. Clark, William, 1770–1838—Juvenile literature. 2. Lewis, Meriwether, 1774–1809—Juvenile literature. 3. Explorers—West (U.S.)—Biography—Juvenile literature. 4. Lewis and Clark Expedition (1804–1806)—Juvenile literature. 5. West (U.S.)—Discovery and exploration—Juvenile literature. [1. Lewis, Meriwether, 1774–1809. 2. Clark, William, 1770–1838. 3. Explorers. 4. Lewis and Clark Expedition (1804–1806) 5. West (U.S.)—Discovery and exploration.] I. Title: William Clark and Meriwether Lewis. II. Noyed, Robert B. III. Title.
   F592.7.C565 K58 2003
   917.804'2'0922—dc21

                              2001007397

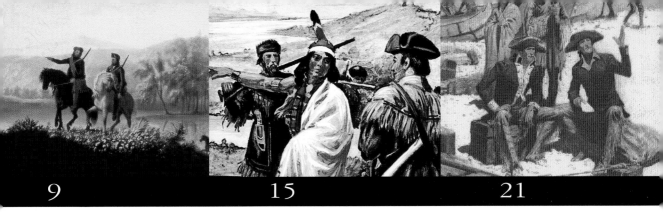

9   15   21

Contents

Chapter ONE

Organizing an Expedition

Sending an expedition to explore the western frontier was President Thomas Jefferson's idea.

IN THE EARLY 1800S, MOST PEOPLE IN THE United States lived in the eastern part of the country. Very little was known about the western **frontier**. President Thomas Jefferson asked Meriwether Lewis and William Clark to explore this new land. The exploration became known as the Lewis and Clark **expedition**.

Meriwether Lewis was born on August 18, 1774, in Virginia. He grew up on a large **plantation** there. Lewis joined the Virginia **militia** in 1794 and the U.S. Army in 1795. He became a captain in 1800. In early 1801, President Jefferson appointed Lewis to be his private secretary.

Lewis and Jefferson shared a vision for exploring the West. It is no surprise that Jefferson asked Lewis to help lead the expedition to the west. To prepare Lewis for the expedition, Jefferson sent him to Philadelphia, Pennsylvania, for a month. There, Lewis learned a great deal about history, plants, rocks, animals, and astronomy.

Meriwether Lewis was President Jefferson's private secretary.

William Clark was the other leader of the expedition. Clark was born in Virginia on August 1, 1770. All of Clark's five brothers had fought in the Revolutionary War (1775–1783). Clark joined the U.S. Army in 1789 and fought in several battles against Native American tribes. Clark met Meriwether Lewis in the army and the two became good friends.

Lewis suggested to President Jefferson that William Clark join the expedition. He knew Clark's skills as a mapmaker, artist, and writer would be helpful. Clark would keep

Interesting Fact

▸ Thomas Jefferson called the expedition the "Corps of Discovery."

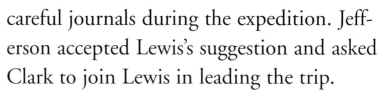
William Clark became friends with Meriwether Lewis in the U.S. Army.

careful journals during the expedition. Jefferson accepted Lewis's suggestion and asked Clark to join Lewis in leading the trip.

By the time both Lewis and Clark had agreed to take part in the exploration, the United States had bought the vast Louisiana Territory from France. The **treaty**, which became known as the Louisiana Purchase, covered more than 825,000 square miles (2,136,750 square kilometers). Lewis and Clark were the first official explorers of this new land.

In the fall of 1803, Lewis and Clark traveled by boat down the Ohio River. They went up the Mississippi River to the mouth of the Missouri River. They spent the winter here making final preparations for their expedition.

Lewis and Clark were not sure what they would find on their journey. They knew they would have to travel through the Rocky Mountains. They also knew they would need help from the Indians to travel

through Indian Territory. The trip would be challenging, to say the least.

Lewis and Clark set off with about 45 men. These men were picked for a variety of skills. Some were skilled hunters and woodcutters, and some were craftspeople. Others could speak different languages.

After much preparation, the Lewis and Clark expedition was ready to begin. It would be an exciting journey.

A painting of Meriwether Lewis and William Clark on their expedition from St. Louis to the Pacific Ocean

IN THE LATE 1700s, THE LAND WEST OF THE MISSISSIPPI RIVER DID NOT belong to the United States. It had been handed over from Spain to France. In 1800, France gained control of this vast area from the Mississippi River west to the Rocky Mountains (right). It was called Louisiana Territory.

The United States needed the Mississippi River. Boats carried people and supplies between the north and south. It was also a way to reach the sea. Spain had allowed the United States to use the river as needed.

France and the United States did not get along well at this time, however. Thomas Jefferson, the president of the United States, was afraid that France would not allow Americans to use the Mississippi River. This would make travel and trade very difficult.

Jefferson decided that the United States had to find a way to buy this huge area of land from France. But Congress approved only $2 million to buy the land!

After many discussions, the United States reached an agreement with the French government. France would sell the land to the United States—for about $15 million. They signed a treaty called the Louisiana Purchase. In one day, the size of the United States doubled.

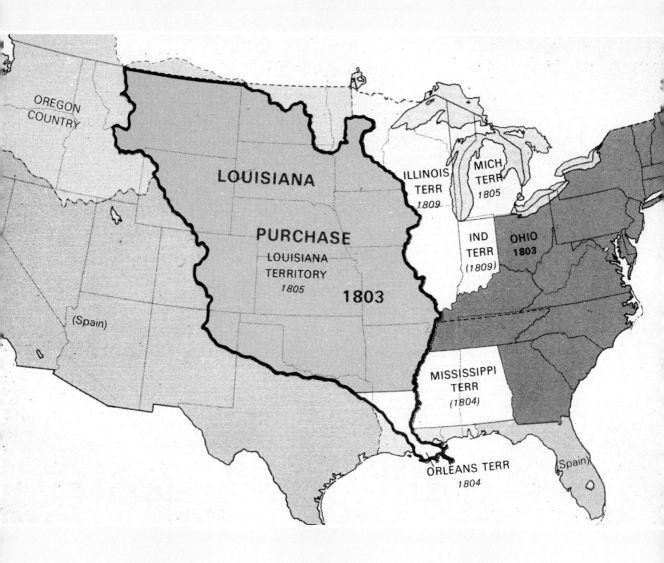

OREGON
COUNTRY

LOUISIANA

PURCHASE

LOUISIANA
TERRITORY
1805

1803

(Spain)

ILLINOIS
TERR
1809

MICH
TERR
1805

IND
TERR
(1809)

OHIO
1803

MISSISSIPPI
TERR
(1804)

ORLEANS TERR
1804

Spain)

Chapter Two

Setting Off

THE GREAT ADVENTURE, FIRST IMAGINED BY Thomas Jefferson, was ready to begin. The Lewis and Clark expedition left the camp near St. Louis, Missouri, on May 14, 1804.

The group set off with three boats—a **keelboat** and two large dugout canoes. The men rowed and sailed against the current of

The expedition set off from St. Louis.

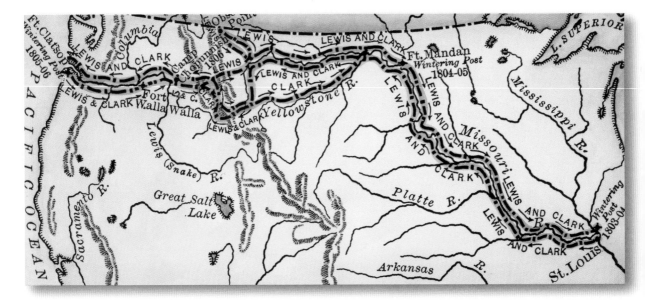

the wide and powerful Missouri River. They had to watch out for sandbars and tree branches floating in the river.

In those early days on the river, they often met trappers loaded with furs. They were rugged men who knew the river and the land. Clark asked a trapper named Pierre Dorion to go north with them to help them communicate with the Sioux Indians. Dorion agreed to go with the expedition.

The explorers met many fur trappers.

As they traveled north, the explorers met many Native American tribes. They had a peaceful encounter with a band of Yankton Sioux. Less friendly tribes waited for them up river, however.

At the end of September, the expedition ran into a group of Teton Sioux. The Teton Sioux blocked their path and demanded gifts and supplies. Lewis and Clark refused, but

Interesting Fact

▶ When Lewis and Clark reached Great Falls on the Missouri River, it was considered their greatest discovery.

13

the Teton Sioux finally allowed the explorers to pass anyway.

In October 1804, the expedition reached a Mandan Indian village in North Dakota. The weather was beginning to get rough. Light snow was already falling. The explorers quickly built a fort and prepared to spend the winter.

They soon had visitors at Fort Mandan. A burly French-Canadian trapper named Toussaint Charbonneau and his Shoshone wife—Sacagawea (sah-kuh-juh-WEE-uh)—came to the fort. Charbonneau was looking for work, so the expedition hired him as an interpreter.

Lewis and Clark were interested in Sacagawea's stories. She told them about secret Indian trails through the mountains. She also promised to help Lewis and Clark get horses from the Shoshone people. The explorers needed horses to cross the Rocky Mountains.

That winter, Sacagawea gave birth to a baby boy named Jean Baptiste. When spring came, she and her baby left with the explorers.

A Teton Sioux chief

Sacagawea did her best to help the expedition. She befriended the Indian tribes they met along the way. Many Indian warriors were curious about the purpose of the expedition. But when they saw Sacagawea and her baby, they realized that the expedition was not a war party and did not attack the group.

The expedition stopped at a Mandan village in North Dakota for the winter.

The expedition continued on its way to the western frontier. Sacagawea continued to be an important member of the group.

At times, young Sacagawea helped guide the group through Native American lands.

PRESIDENT THOMAS JEFFERSON WAS IN OFFICE DURING THE LEWIS and Clark expedition. His great interest in nature was part of the reason he wanted to learn more about the new lands west of the Mississippi.

Thomas Jefferson was born on April 13, 1743, on his family's large farm in Virginia. The farm covered more than 1,000 acres (405 ha) at the edge of the wilderness.

Jefferson had many interests. He designed houses and buildings, including his own home, called Monticello (opposite), in 1768. He studied plants, shrubs, and trees. He played the violin. He was also an enthusiastic reader and an excellent writer.

In addition to serving as the third U.S. president, Jefferson played another important role in the history of the United States. He wrote the first draft of the Declaration of Independence—the document that declared the country's freedom from Britain. It also expressed the ideas that served as the basis for the government of the United States.

Chapter THREE

Ocean in View

In one famous story, Meriwether Lewis shot the expedition's first grizzly bear just after crossing into North Dakota.

IN MAY 1805, THE LEWIS AND CLARK EXPEDITION was traveling across Montana. Lewis and Clark saw many elk, deer, and antelope. They also saw animals that they had never seen before. At one point, a large grizzly bear attacked Lewis and another hunter. Lewis killed the bear and they wrote in their journals about what they had seen.

A serious boat accident almost ruined the trip. A strong wind came up and one of the dugout canoes tipped over. That boat contained all the expedition's

papers, books, medicines, and scientific instruments. Luckily, the canoe did not sink. Sacagawea almost drowned in the accident, but she helped to save the equipment.

Traveling by canoe could be dangerous.

In late July 1805, the explorers approached the Three Forks of the Missouri River. Sacagawea told Lewis and Clark that they were near her tribe's hunting grounds. Two weeks later, Lewis and a few other men met with a Shoshone chief named Cameahwait. Clark, Sacagawea, and the rest of the party followed a few days later. Sacagawea was excited when she saw the chief—he was her brother!

Cameahwait told Lewis and Clark that high mountains lay just ahead. He warned them that winter came early in the mountains and there were few animals to hunt. The chief gave the explorers 29 horses and a mule. He also sent Indian guides along to lead them through the mountains.

Interesting Fact

▸ The explorers carried 12 dozen pocket mirrors, 144 small scissors, 130 rolls of tobacco, and 8 brass kettles to give as gifts to the Native Americans.

Meriwether Lewis gets his first look at the Rocky Mountains.

The explorers set out through the mountains on August 30, 1805. By September 16, however, the trail was already deep in snow, and the party was running out of food. They nearly starved while crossing the mountains. After a dreadful journey, they arrived in the land of the Nez Percé Indians. Luckily, the Nez Percé people were friendly. They told Lewis and Clark that the Columbia River was a week's journey to the west.

The explorers made dugout canoes and began their journey to the Columbia River. They sailed down the Clearwater River to the Snake River. The water was rough and they had to paddle through many dangerous rapids. Finally, on October 16, they reached the Columbia River. Lewis and Clark knew they were close to reaching the coast of the ocean.

On November 7, 1805, Clark wrote in his journal, "Ocean in view! Oh, the joy!" The expedition was still about 20 miles (32 kilometers) from the ocean, however. After weeks of stormy weather, the group finally crossed the Columbia River and arrived on the Oregon coast.

In this drawing by Frederic Remington, Lewis and Clark celebrate their arrival at the mouth of the Columbia River.

The explorers had reached their destination. They built a settlement near the coast and called it Fort Clatsop after the Clatsop Indians in the area. The fort became the expedition's winter home.

Near the Pacific coast, members of the expedition built Fort Clatsop.

SACAGAWEA GREW UP IN THE SHOSHONE TRIBE. LIFE FOR SHOSHONE girls and women was not always pleasant. They worked hard and were often mistreated.

When Sacagawea was about 12 years old, Hidatsa Indians attacked her tribe and captured Sacagawea. They later sold her as a slave to the Missouri River Mandan people. They lived in what is now North Dakota. Her life there was one of hard work and mistreatment. One night, a French-Canadian man named Toussaint Charbonneau was gambling with some of the Mandan Indians. His winnings included Sacagawea and she was forced to marry him. They lived in the Mandan village until they joined the expedition.

When their expedition ended, Lewis and Clark wanted to pay Sacagawea for her help. Clark and Sacagawea agreed that Clark would raise Sacagawea's son and provide him with a good education and everything needed to be successful in the white man's society. Jean Baptiste became well educated and later served as the mayor of San Luis Rey, California.

No one is sure how or when Sacagawea died. One story says she caught a deadly illness and died at Fort Manuel in 1812. Another story says she joined the Shoshone people and died in 1884, when she was almost 100 years old.

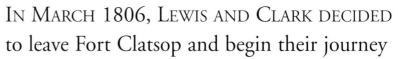

Chapter FOUR

Return and Reward

The expedition made a trail through the Bitterroot Range.

IN MARCH 1806, LEWIS AND CLARK DECIDED to leave Fort Clatsop and begin their journey back to Missouri. They gave the fort to the Clatsop Indians and left on their long trip home.

As they traveled east, the explorers crossed the Bitterroot Range. The Nez Percé people helped them greatly. Before crossing the mountains, the group stayed with the Nez Percé until the snow melted in the mountains. In his journal, Lewis called the Nez Percé "the most hospitable, honest and sincere people we have met with in our voyage."

After they crossed the mountains, the explorers split into groups in order to cover more territory. Clark, Sacagawea, and most of the men went south. They explored the Yellowstone River and part of Montana. Near what is now Billings, Montana, Clark discovered a stone outcropping. He named it Pompey's Tower, after Sacagawea's little boy, Jean Baptiste, whose nickname was Little Pomp. Clark carved his name into the rock.

Meanwhile, Lewis and a small group of men went north. Lewis and his group soon met up with eight Blackfoot warriors. They camped together, but a fight broke out when the Indians tried to steal Lewis's horses and guns.

The two groups met again on August 12

A Blackfoot warrior

25

near the mouth of the Yellowstone River. They traveled together to the Mandan village in North Dakota. The expedition said a sad good-bye to Charbonneau, Sacagawea, and Jean Baptiste, who stayed at the Mandan village.

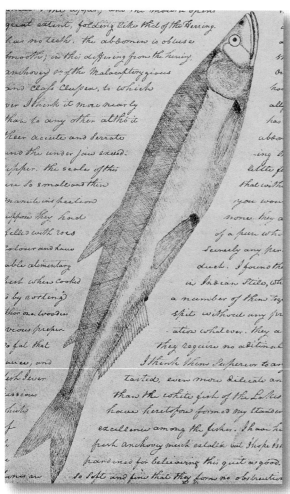

A sketch of a trout from William Clark's journal

After sailing for about a month, Lewis and Clark reached St. Louis on September 23, 1806. Their expedition was over, and it was a great success. They had traveled more than 7,600 miles (12,228 km) and discovered new territory for the United States.

Lewis and Clark were now considered national heroes. In Washington, D.C., they were honored by President Jefferson for their work. All the expedition members received double pay and 320 acres (130 ha) of land. Lewis and Clark were each given 1,600 acres (648 ha) of land.

Lewis was then appointed governor of Louisiana Territory. He was supposed to start this job in March 1807.

After Lewis went to Washington, D.C., to collect his rewards for the expedition, he traveled to Philadelphia. He was looking for someone to publish his and Clark's journals from the expedition. He finally arrived in St. Louis in March 1808 to take over as governor—more than a year late.

Lewis had difficulty trying to govern the new territory. In September 1809, he left St. Louis for a trip to Washington, D.C. Along the way, Lewis probably became depressed and took his own life. However, some historians believe Lewis was murdered. He was just 35 years old when he died.

After the expedition, President Jefferson named Clark **brigadier general** of militia for

The gravestone of Meriwether Lewis stands on an old pioneer road called the Natchez Trace in Tennessee.

27

Louisiana Territory. In 1813, he was appointed governor of Missouri Territory. Clark also served as **superintendent** of Indian Affairs. In that position, he tried to help all Native American people. Clark died on September 1, 1838, in St. Louis, at age 68, having lived a long and productive life.

The Lewis and Clark expedition is still remembered as one of the most important expeditions in U.S. history. It helped open up the western frontier.

William Clark lived for many years after Meriwether Lewis's death.

Time LINE

LOUISIANA PURCHASE
LOUISIANA TERRITORY 1805

ILLINOIS TERR 1809

1803

MERIWETHER LEWIS

1800   1805   1809

1770 William Clark is born on August 1 in Virginia.

1774 Meriwether Lewis is born on August 18 in Virginia.

1789 Clark joins the U.S. Army.

1794 Lewis joins the Virginia militia.

1795 Lewis joins the U.S. Army.

1800 Lewis becomes a U.S. Army captain.

1801 President Jefferson appoints Lewis to be his private secretary.

1803 Lewis and Clark spend the winter in a camp near St. Louis preparing for the trip.

1804 The Lewis and Clark expedition sets out on the Missouri River on May 14. In October, they reach a Mandan Indian village in North Dakota and prepare to spend the winter.

1805 Lewis and Clark hire an interpreter named Charbonneau, who brings his wife Sacagawea and son Jean Baptiste. In May, the explorers travel across Montana. In July, they approach Three Forks on the Missouri River. In August,

they meet a Shoshone chief named Cameahwait, who turns out to be Sacagawea's brother. On August 30, the group sets out to cross the mountains. On October 16, they reach the Columbia River. In November, they reach the Pacific Ocean and build Fort Clatsop.

1806 In March, Lewis and Clark leave Fort Clatsop on their return trip. After crossing the Bitterroot Range, the expedition splits into groups to explore more territory. On August 12, the two groups meet again near the mouth of the Yellowstone River. They travel to the Mandan village in North Dakota, where Charbonneau, Sacagawea, and Jean Baptiste leave the expedition. On September 23, Lewis and Clark reach St. Louis.

1808 Lewis is named governor of Louisiana Territory.

1809 Meriwether Lewis dies on October 11 in Tennessee.

1813 Clark is appointed governor of Missouri Territory.

1838 William Clark dies on September 1 in St. Louis, Missouri.

**brigadier general
(brih-guh-DEER JEN-ruhl)**
A brigadier general is a military officer below a major general in rank. William Clark served as brigadier general of militia for Louisiana Territory.

expedition (ek-spuh-DISH-uhn)
An expedition is a long journey for a special purpose. President Thomas Jefferson asked Lewis and Clark to explore the northwest territory of the United States. The word expedition can also be used to describe the group that makes the journey.

frontier (frun-TIHR)
A frontier is the far edge of a settled land, where few people live. The Lewis and Clark expedition explored the western frontier of the United States.

keelboat (KEEL-boht)
A keelboat is a large boat with a flat bottom and a covered deck. The Lewis and Clark expedition set off in a keelboat and two large dugout canoes.

militia (muh-LISH-uh)
A militia is a group of citizens trained to fight in emergencies. Meriwether Lewis was a member of the Virginia militia.

plantation (plan-TAY-shuhn)
A plantation is a large farm. Meriwether Lewis grew up on a plantation in Virginia.

superintendent (SOO-pur-in-TEN-dunt)
A superintendent is someone who manages an organization. William Clark served as superintendent of Indian Affairs.

treaty (TREE-tee)
A treaty is an agreement between two governments. In the treaty known as the Louisiana Purchase, the United States bought Louisiana Territory from France for $15 million.

For Further INFORMATION

Web Sites

Visit our homepage for lots of links about Lewis and Clark:
http://www.childsworld.com/links.html

Note to Parents, Teachers, and Librarians:
We routinely verify our Web links to make sure they're safe,
active sites—so encourage your readers to check them out!

Books

Clark, William, and Peter and Connie Roop, eds. *Off the Map: The Journals of Lewis and Clark.* New York: Walker and Company, 1993.

Patent, Dorothy Hinshaw. *Animals on the Trail with Lewis and Clark.* New York: Clarion Books, 2002.

Schanzer, Rosalyn. *How We Crossed the West: The Adventures of Lewis & Clark.* Washington, D.C.: National Geographic Society, 1997.

Sullivan, George. *Lewis and Clark.* New York: Scholastic, 2000.

Places to Visit or Contact

Lewis & Clark National Historic Trail Interpretive Center
To see exhibits about expedition life
4201 Giant Springs Road
Great Falls, MT 59403
406-727-8733

Fort Clatsop National Memorial
To visit the site of the original fort
92343 Fort Clatsop Road
Astoria, OR 97103-9197
503-861-2471

31

Index